The Journey Continues:
More Poetry of an Immigrant

By Peter Murray

year of publication 2011
written in Canada

All contents of this book are copyrighted to Peter Murray

This book is dedicated to the memory of my mother, whom I never appreciated as much as I should when she was alive. Much of my memories of her may have been stolen but all my love and gratitude remain.

I miss you

Thanks and acknowledgments:

Thanks to my family for putting up with my constant asking to read the draft copies of my book, this time I will not make the silly mistakes I did in my last book.

A special thanks to the creators of Open Office, a free word processor is a low-budget authors best friend, please keep up the good work.

Contents

Sleep	9
The Sentient Being	11
Dying Planet	13
Battered Fish	15
The Painter	17
The Play	19
A Poetic Self-portrait	21
A Special Person	23
Niagara Falls	25
Shattered Glass	27
Corner View of Freedom	29
Blank Page	31
Michelle	33
Job Start	35
Too Many Questions	37
WWW	39
Fallen Soldier	41
Wet Morning	43
Error's Comedy	45
Guy Fawkes	47
Fugitive	49
All For Nothing	51
Sunshine Through The Window	53
Hazel	55
The Perfect World	57
Elusive Future	59
The Lines Of The Road	61
Ballad Of The Push-iron	63
Auschwitz	65
At Book's End	67

Sleep

Hello my bed, my trusted friend,
You are always at days end,
your spongy mattress holds me soft,
above your springs, held aloft,
Gently I drift into a blissful slumber,
after counting sheep, too many to number,
here I lay dreaming away,
in a few hours it will be another day.

The Sentient Being

A sentient being watches silently,
high above a planet acting violently,
on the ever changing world we scurry around,
never a thought to things far above the ground,
one day we all will see we are not alone,
we are not the only ones to call this planet home,
but how, choose we, to greet our guests?
Please not with guns and metal chests,
for every sentient being deserves a chance,
to present itself in a friendly stance,
let us not engage in a bloody war,
for we have come to a point where we need no more.

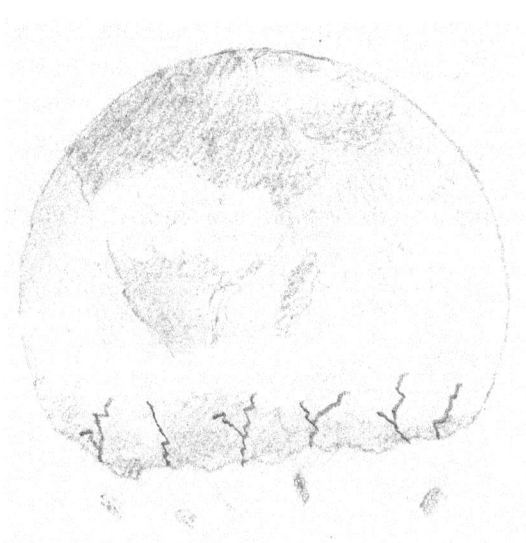

Dying Planet

I look out of my windows at world I see,
I find my self begging, "please, do not let this be!",
my planet is now in turmoil,
toxic has become its once fertile soil,
but where do we go when,
the plants no longer grow as they did then,
we may not be able to destroy this planet,
but we can certainly kill all the people on it.
It may not be too late,
to try out best and clean the slate,
and once again we can live free,
in a happy world for you and me.

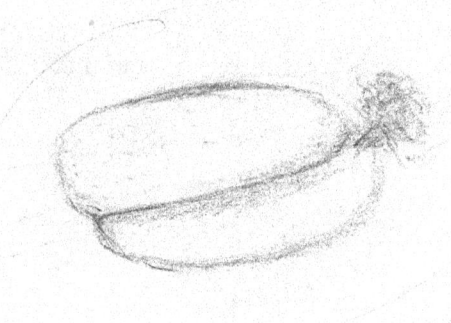

Battered Fish

It's almost time for the dinner hour,
so I take one cup of all-purpose flour,
one-half teaspoon of baking powder,
distant sounds of stomachs grow louder,
I add some salt, about a quarter teaspoon,
heat up some oil, we will be frying soon,
pour in one cup of fresh milk,
mix it up 'till as smooth as silk,
with loving care, coat your fish,
after a few minutes of frying,
you will have a traditional English dish.

The Painter

On a hillside a lonely painter sits,
with brush in hand, beautiful images he emits,
at each stroke, the picture slowly becomes clear,
a rolling countryside and several large deer,
the master continues to develop his work,
pristine images appearing from murk,
when is captured landscape has become complete,
he will look back at this feat,
then he shall hang it in a gallery for all to see,
or give it as a gift to the local marquis.

The Play

A play, fit for the bard, was performed today,
the crown all cheered and clapped in the usual way,
the actors all come to take their final bow,
it was certainly entertaining, and how,
I came tonight expecting a bore,
but now will last in my memory forever more,
Oh, I wish this play would never finish,
or the music to ever diminish,
but alas, the end has come to this night,
acta est fabula plaudite

A Poetic Self-portrait

A strange tall man, with a ginger beard,
likes to write poetry, he is a bit weird,
he has eyes that sparkle a dark shade of blue,
in hand a cup of tea, his favourite brew,
you would hear him before seeing him out on the street,
with his enormous stomach and size thirteen feet,
do not think this poem is to insult,
for you might be surprised to find out the result,
to make you thing of who it could be?
It is the author of this poem, it is me.

A Special Person

A special person knows when they are wrong,
not the type who would just bite their tongue,
they would admit their mistakes,
accept the consequences it makes,
then continue their life with a clear mind.
To be a special person takes dedication and time,
working towards a goal and not turning to crime.
Some things in life are harder than others,
it can sometimes break our backs to please our mothers,
but honesty and kindness are the best approach,
taking only what's yours, never to poach.
You can look back on your life,
when years have long since passed,
and count the good deeds that you have amassed.

Niagara Falls

Water falls off the wall of jagged rocks,
with strength many hundred times that of an ox,
the mist rises up all around,
everything deafened by the roaring sound,
The Maid of the Mist sails wearily through,
giving some tourists a pleasant view,
they go in dry then come out wet,
as if sprayed with a water jet.
People flock from throughout the world,
to watch these thousands of litres hurled.
This beautiful scene hides it's great peril,
which becomes clear if you ride it in a barrel.
Thousands of years old is the water flow,
creating this fantastic natural show,
if you have not seen this wonderful sight,
then I suggest heavily that you book that flight.

Shattered Glass

Shards of a crystal figure lay motionless on the floor,
it's delicately sculptured beauty to be seen no more,
the pieces glisten all day in the sunlight,
they remain there 'till the night,
memories of this item sitting peacefully in the hall,
destroyed in seconds against the wall,
tears of anger with screams of rage,
the worst of our emotions take front stage,
but with sudden sound of the shattered glass,
sadness appears, violent emotions pass,
now overcome with remorse and bitter regret,
left with the mound of debris from which they beget,
with the slam of the door,
a marriage no more,
weeps are heard from a figure in the corner,
slouched against the wall, heart ripped from her.

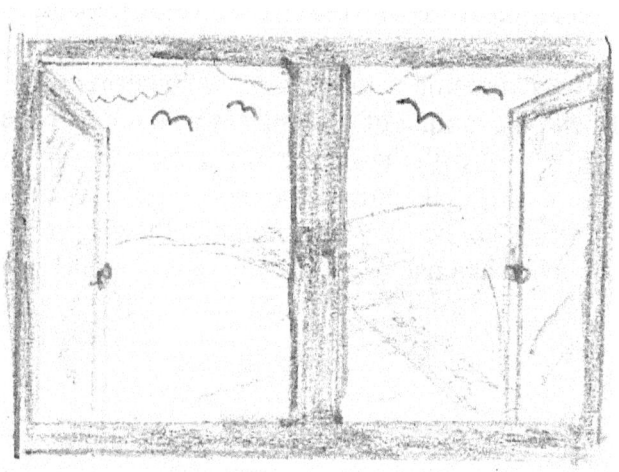

Corner View of Freedom

I stand lonely in the corner,
feeling a little like Jack Horner,
except when I pull out my thumb,
I don't see a shining plum.
I watch the world passing by,
I see the planes flying in the sky.
A train goes by in the distance,
birds soar by with no resistance,
off it flies to destinations unknown,
places special to it alone.
I am like that bird,
wishing to be never seen or heard,
one day I shall be free,
and that will be the last you see of me.

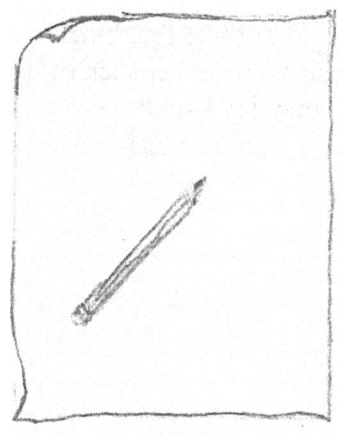

Blank Page

O piece of paper sitting on my desk,
your lack of writing looks quite grotesque,
I should take a pen and write some words,
or maybe even scribble pictures of several birds.
The paper is a mirror of my vacant mind,
void of memories left behind,
only if I could find some small detail,
I can get this train of life back on it's rail.
For now I will just sit and stare,
at the piece paper siting there,
until the day it all comes back,
then with the scribbles I hang it with a tack,
on the wall of my life,
displaying the fruit of endless strife.

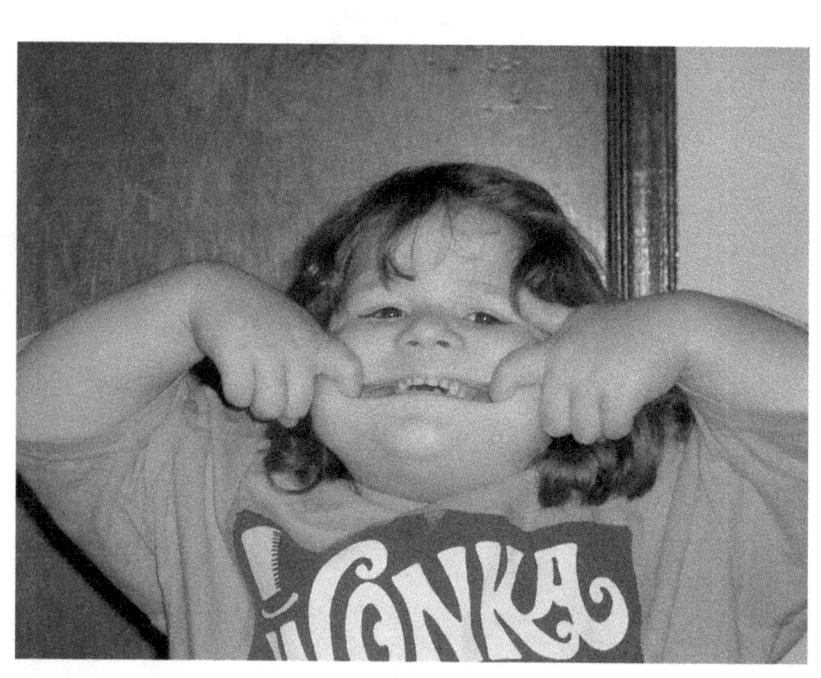

Michelle

She makes the sun shine every single day,
when she smiles she pushes the clouds away,
Without her, my life has no meaning,
her charms require no preening,
for you, I have forgone days of sleep,
a love for you that is deep,
no one can understand how special you are to me,
to leave or abandon you, that could never be,
one day you will look back on this time,
even though it may be a long time,
and remember all the good things,
treasure the memories they bring,
cherish my words, cherish my love,
they are what this life is made of,
for you I would sacrifice everything,
no matter how much it would sting,
until my job is complete,
I will remain by your side,
I will not run, I will not hide,
being your father is my greatest feat.

I have never and will never regret it.

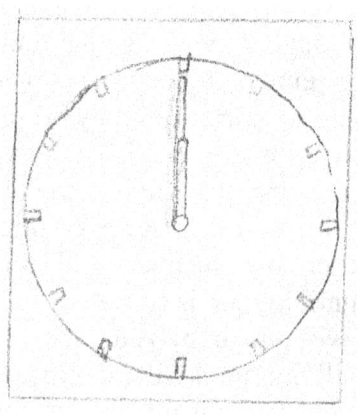

Job Start

As the hands of the clock race around it's face,
another day will begin with a startling pace,
the glory and splendor is a product of dreams,
my brain stuffed full of information, bursting at it's seams,
thirteen hours until my start,
hopefully soon, I'll have it down to an art,
and then the task will become routine,
like a daily helping of fresh poutine,
Work is the fries, I am the cheese,
hopefully with the gravy, all will be at ease,
thirteen more hours to go,
how it will be, I do not know.

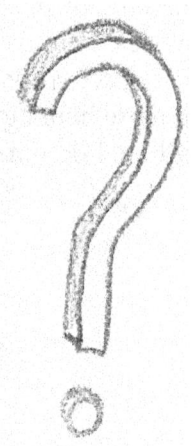

Too Many Questions

How many cars do you see in a day?
How many singers perform in a play?
How many words do I have take to say?
How many reasons do I need to stay?
How many times can we continue this way?
How many tugs until this rope will fray?
How many sheep can we count on the brae?
How many verses in the prayer that I pray?
How many stones do I need to weigh?
How many cats and dog are alone and stray?
How many bricks can be made from a ton of clay?
How many walls can we paint shades of grey?
How many horses can we hear that bray?
How many hurtful attacks do I have to receive from they?
Life is but full of mysteries and strife,
but if all is answered what would be left to do in life?

WWW

Welcome to the world of the world wide web,
were data moves in a high speed flow and ebb,
think of it as one large city,
full of lights and splendor, the face is pretty,
but be aware of the darkened alleys,
stay clear of the hidden valleys,
for there lives the underworld of this place,
in these places you can disappear without a trace,
as with every city you will find places of conflict,
and an area called the red light district,
travel this city with tremendous care,
don't get tempted with all the flair,
find yourself a good guide,
or you could end up on an unpleasant ride.

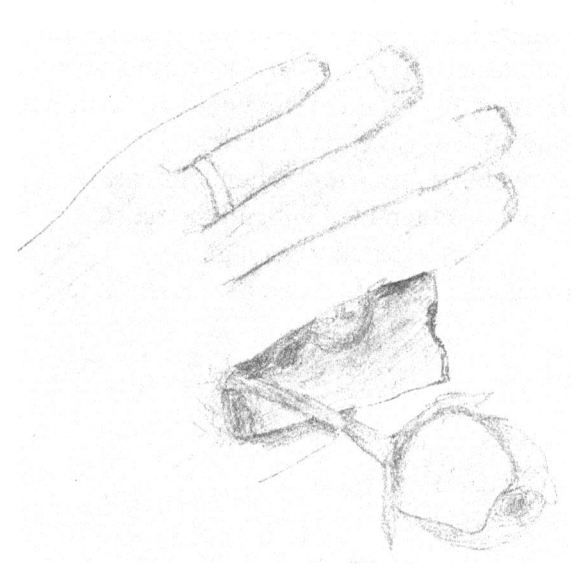

Fallen Soldier

In a distant field grows a rose,
it's beauty, from the ground which it owes,
the rose sways with a gentle class,
in the wind that blows across the grass,
before long, war comes to this land,
booms are heard as if from a band,
a fallen soldier reaches for the rose,
with his blood soaked hand, shaking with dread
he uproots the rose from it's soil bed,
with cries of pain, he kisses the rose,
and with his wife's photo, he holds it close,
his silent tears trickle down face,
very much alone, in much need of grace
knowing he will never see his love again,
the tears continue to fall, like the continuing rain.
In a distant field, lies a dying young man,
under a sky of a cloudy dull cyan,
now fading with the last flickers of life,
taken in seconds with the sting of a trench knife.

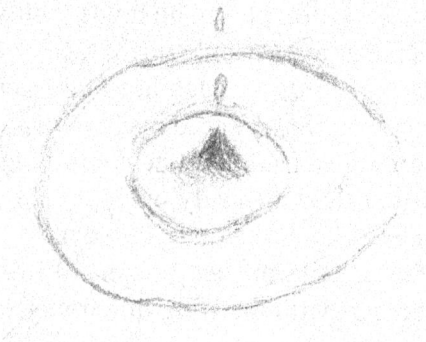

Wet Morning

I awake to find a sky of grey,
predicted for me, a rainy day,
I leave the house with my rain coat,
the depressing weather like a lump in my throat,
it's not long before the rain begins to fall,
drips pattering on my head make me feel small,
I start to walk through the park,
it's very early in the morning, it is still dark,
I walk past the pond and watch the ripples,
they race across the water in doubles and triples,
they silently rebound at the bank,
like bubbles in a tropical fish tank,
in the distance the dawn begins to break,
I hear the morning chorus being lead by a drake,
all the sounds around, nature has spoken,
good morning world, a new day has broken.

Error's Comedy

There was once a young man called Tony,
A Jinx of sorts, this guy could crash a pony,
the legend is he had a strange knack,
the uncanny ability to kernel panic a new mac,
his exploits happen on a daily basis,
bring joy and laughter to the many faces,
coming faster than a roller coaster,
he's able to burn pizza in a toaster,
despite being well built and burly,
he's occasional in the need of a swirley,
being a modern Jonah we could not ask for more,
this is why he's the inspiration for team 404.

Guy Fawkes

It's early November again,
you can tell by the freezing rain,
fireworks explode in the background,
a bonfire with people standing around,
Guido's effigy burns motionless in the fire,
four centuries old reminder to those who conspire.
The plot to blow up the brick and cement,
of the building of the parliament,
was a very revolutionary thing,
especially when it was attended by the king,
but instead Guy was fatally betrayed,
which ended with his burning body
unceremoniously publicly displayed.

Fugitive

A man stands quietly in a room,
silently contemplating his doom,
police sirens blaring in the street,
many armed men up on their feet,
choices have all but run out,
a painful decision that comes with a shout,
a burst of gun fire and a man is now dead,
situation ended by a bullet through the head,
he chose this to be the way he would die,
the police outside would have preferred him to fry,
for his crimes against humanity we quite severe,
the price to pay for those crimes was very dear,
no matter how you hide from you past my friend,
it will always track you down and catch up in the end.

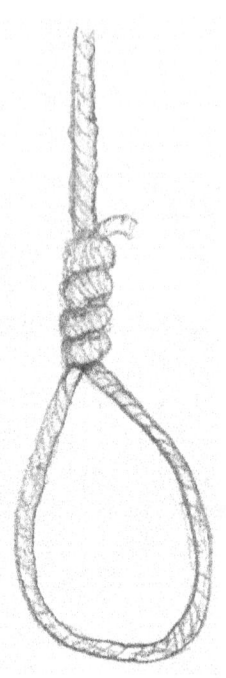

All For Nothing

Off into the night,
a shapeless shadow takes flight,
taking with it the very last part,
from the pieces of my shattered heart.
Spiraling down a filthy toilet,
are the parts the shadows could not get,
screams are all that remain inside of my head,
making me wish that I was dead,
my life in ruins, I contemplate my choices,
and try to find a solution with the least noises.
In the end I dangle above my bed,
suspended from noose ended thread.

Sunshine Through The Window

I see her smile through the window's glass,
elegant, intelligent, with a certain class.
I saw you yesterday, maybe tomorrow,
if I don't, it may cause me sorrow.
When you are near, singing can be heard,
a sweet melody like only comes from a bird,
I see the sun is shining in the sky,
it must mean you're near, I don't know why.
These silly little things help my day smoothly pass,
such a special person, defiantly not crass,
but one day soon, you shall be gone,
and I will be left, a lonely one,
but lets not thing about that day,
and please let it not be today,
for when I no longer see you there,
my days will be empty and completely bare.

Hazel

I see her sleeping silently in her bed,
I wonder what dreams go through her head,
this is one of the things I'll never know,
laying there so quietly, lights down low,
Temping as it is, to touch your soft brown hair,
but I don't want to disturb you from laying there,
the time we have is all so precious,
it's enough to make anyone jealous,
but alas once again I must leave for the day,
I'll return again later, then for the night I will stay,
but in the end I will miss you when your gone,
it will be hard but I will find the strength to carry on.

The Perfect World

I hear the wind in the trees,
a calming gentle passing breeze,
it's a nice summer day,
lots of sunshine coming my way,
in the distance is the singing of the lark,
and the laughter of children in the park,
it's the perfect world where nobody ever cries,
and there is never a grey cloud in the vast blue skies,
the whole world is at peace,
wandering around as happy as a flock of geese,
maybe one day this will all come true,
and there will be a perfect world for me and you.

Elusive Future

Thoughts of the future are not as they seem,
sometimes they don't go as far as a dream,
you hope to catch up to it all some day,
but somehow it always seems to get away,
you can spend your whole life trying to achieve,
but it get further from you each time you stop to breathe,
then one day you see everything disappear into the sky,
you awake to find a decade has passed you by,
fear not for all that seems to be gone,
for your still alive, and the race is yet to be won.

The Lines Of The Road

I see the lines in the middle of the road,
dotting and dashing, just like Morse code,
we follow these lines throughout our lives,
straight and narrow, as sharp as knives,
rarely do we get a chance to make a detour,
if we do, we can never be sure,
of where about we may end up,
wandering aimlessly, like a lost pup.
These lines we use as our eternal guide,
never knowing if it has ever lied,
but still we continue day by day,
no one know what direction the future will sway.

Ballad Of The Push-iron

To ride a bike is to be free on two wheels,
it's amazing to those who know how good it feels,
to speed down a hill,
it is such a thrill,
it's like flying without leaving the ground,
zipping along with very little sound,
the freedom of the road on a tyres and spokes,
sometimes being at the centre of jokes,
but I will never give up the wind through my hair,
and continue riding with my passion and flair.

Auschwitz

The horror, the dread,
the screams from the dead,
several living skeletons, all restricted to a bed,
incarceration in conditions unspeakably grim,
the light in their eyes now glowing very dim,
a hut full of people in their striped and tattered suits,
all brought together to be punished for their roots,
it should never have happened and should never again,
all the innocent people who were arbitrarily slain,
if history has taught use one lesson for sure,
there is no such thing as one race being pure,
may the sins of the past haunt the guilty one's sleep,
and be a warning to those who follow like sheep.

In memory of Johann Karlsson Brasse
survivor of Auschwitz

At Book's End

Time has come to end this book,
to check all the spelling and wish it luck,
in a few days it will be off to publish,
hoping I've not missed any mistakes that are foolish,
in a few weeks it will go to the book store,
where I hope it sells so I can write more,
for the only thing about being a poet,
is it's time consuming and don't I know it!
All the thoughts are expressed into text,
now I shall think about what will come next,
thinking of stories, anything I can lend,
but for now this is it, we're at book's end.